Health and My Body

Limit Screen Time

by Martha E. H. Rustad

PEBBLE
a capstone imprint

Pebble Explore is published by Pebble, an imprint of Capstone
1710 Roe Crest Drive
North Mankato, Minnesota 56003
www.capstonepub.com

**Library of Congress Cataloging-in-Publication Data is available on
the Library of Congress website.**
ISBN: 978-1-9771-2385-5 (library binding)
ISBN: 978-1-9771-2685-6 (paperback)
ISBN: 978-1-9771-2422-7 (eBook PDF)
Summary: Devices with screens are all around us. But too much time
on these devices can be unhealthy. Learn how to cut the screen time.

Image Credits
iStockphoto: Bhupi, 9, FlairImages, 26; Shutterstock: Africa Studio,
15, Bacho, 18, bbernard, 28, Diego Cervo, 16, dragon_fang, 17,
Hasnuddin, 24, Iakov Filimonov, 12, imtmphoto, 5, Joshua Resnick,
25, mattomedia KG, 23, Monkey Business Images, 10, 21, MPH
Photos, 4, Mr.Note19, 29, Patrick Foto, 14, photonova, design element
throughout, TinnaPong, 7, wavebreakmedia, Cover, 13

Editorial Credits
Editor: Michelle Parkin; Designer: Sarah Bennett; Media Researcher:
Morgan Walters; Production Specialist: Laura Manthe

All internet sites appearing in back matter were available and
accurate when this book was sent to press.

Printed in the United States of America.
PA117

Table of Contents

Bold words are in the glossary.

Screens Are Everywhere

We watch shows on TV. We play games on smartphones. We read books on **E-readers**. **Devices** with screens are everywhere. Computers and TVs have big screens. **Tablets** and smartphones have small screens.

We learn a lot from what we see on screens. We can find out the weather. We learn about people or animals for school reports. We listen to music. We send messages to friends.

What Is Screen Time?

Screen time is the amount of time we spend looking at devices with screens. Too much screen time can be bad for us.

Screens and Your Body

A lot of screen time can hurt your body. Your neck can get sore from looking down at your phone. Your fingers might hurt from pushing buttons while playing a video game.

Your eyes can hurt. You don't blink as often when you are staring at a screen. Your eyes can get dry. They get tired when you watch something for a long time.

Sleeping

Some people like to watch TV at bedtime. But screens can make sleeping hard. Devices have bright lights. They keep us awake. We do not get a good night's sleep.

When you use devices, it's easy to lose track of time. Some games and phone **apps** give you extra points for spending time on them. This can make you want to play even longer.

Sitting Still

You sit still when you use devices with screens. But you shouldn't sit for too long. You need to stay active. Moving your body is an important way to stay healthy.

You don't have to turn off your devices to exercise. See how many jumping jacks you can do during the TV ads. Dance around your room when you reach a new level in your game. Stretch after each video you watch.

Communicating

We use our smartphones and tablets to **communicate**. But sometimes our messages are not understood. Your friend can't hear you laughing in a text message. Your sister can't see you smile in an email.

Talking to others is important. We learn to communicate better. We use our faces to show what we mean. We can't do that with devices.

Setting Limits

Think of screen time as junk food. A little bit is OK, but too much isn't good for you. Your body needs to have healthy food. Your brain needs healthy activities too.

Screens aren't all bad for you.
We can learn new things. But other
activities are better for your body and
brain. It's important to set screen limits
to stay healthy.

How do you get started? First, try limiting screen time during meals. Put your smartphone away when dinner is ready. Turn off the TV at breakfast. Sit at the table with your family. Talk about your day.

Our bodies need sleep to **recharge**. Turn off your screens an hour before you go to sleep. This will tell your brain to get ready to rest. Instead, play a board game with your family before bed. You could also read a book.

At night, charge all your devices outside of your bedroom. The noises and bright lights can wake you up.

Set a time each day to use your devices. When your time is up, turn off the TV. Set down the phone. Some games and phone apps keep track of how long you use them. This will tell you to stop when your screen time is up. You could also set a timer or use your alarm clock.

Get your family involved too! Plan screen-free time for everyone. Find an empty box or basket. During screen-free time, ask everyone to put their devices inside. No touching until the time is over!

Go Screen Free!

The world is a big place. There is so much to see and do. Think of fun activities you can do away from screens. Here are a few ideas to try.

No screen time while the sun shines! Spend time outside. Go for a walk or to a park with your family. Sit near a plant or tree. Think about what makes it grow.

Read every day. Ask a parent to take you to the library. There are lots of books you can check out. Try reading something new. Ask a **librarian** how to get a library card.

Listen to an **audio book**. Find a **podcast** you like. Some podcasts cover science questions. Others tell great stories. Turn on the story. Then, set the device aside.

Write a play or story. Think up a new episode of your favorite show. Act it out with friends. You can even use puppets to tell the story. Use old socks to make your puppet characters.

Make something new. Draw a picture. Cut pictures out of old magazines. Glue them together to make fun artwork.

Try a new recipe. Ask a parent or
grandparent to show you how to cook
a new dish. Share your tasty treat!

Start a neighborhood game night. Get the kids in your neighborhood to play a game of hide and seek. Meet at a park to play together.

Have a dance party with your friends. Ask everyone to pick a song they like. You can even make up new dance moves together.

Plan a scavenger hunt. Hide items around your home. Then, make a list of what is hidden. You can write clues to help the search!

Share Screen Time

Have a family movie night once a week. Talk about what you see in the movie. Cheer on a friend playing a video game.

Screens are part of our world. We use them every day. But remember to put your devices down sometimes.

Talk with your family about other ways to lower screen time. Together, you can make healthy choices for using devices with screens.

Glossary

app (APP)—a program downloaded to computers and phones; app is short for application

audio book (AW-dee-oh BUHK)—a recording of someone reading a book aloud

communicate (kuh-MYOO-nuh-kate)—to pass along thoughts, feelings, or information

device (di-VISSE)—a piece of equipment made to do a certain job

E-reader (Eh REE-dehr)—a handheld device were electronic copies of books, newspapers, and magazines can be read

librarian (lye-BRER-ee-uhn)—a person trained in library science who helps library visitors

podcast (POD-kast)—a program that can be listened to on a computer or other media player

recharge (ri-CHARJ)—to bring back to how it was before

tablet (TAB-let)—a small, portable computer

Read More

Gagne, Tammy. *Smartphones*. Minneapolis: Cody Koala, 2019.

Melmed, Raun. *Timmy's Monster Diary: Screen Time Stress*. Sanger, CA: Familius, 2017.

Rustad, Martha E. H. *Care for Your Body*. North Mankato, MN: Capstone, 2021.

Internet Sites

Fun Outdoor Games
https://www.kidactivities.net/outdoor-games-for-school-age-kids/

Limit Screen Time
https://www.actionforhealthykids.org/activity/limit-screen-time/

Screen-Free Week
https://www.screenfree.org/

Index